# *An Open Door*

*By*

*Grace Lee*

ISBN 9781326125271

2021 by Grace Lee

Cairns-Australia

## ***Other Books***

*Peta, A Magic Cat*

*The Vanishing Chilltoes*

*Roary's Lost Magic*

*Toby Bears Travels*

*Night Voices*

*500 Words*

*Maze of Words*

*It's in the Book*

## Contents

## *Magic*

Magic happens in my world
It happens every day
Magic happens in my world
In every single way,

Magic happens in my world
Life is a beautiful gift
The sunbirds sing at my window
Giving my day a lift
Grace Lee

## *Introduction*

I have divided this book into three parts. The first part comprises some of the unique experiences I have had throughout my life.

As I was growing up, many supernatural incidents seemed to follow me, things such as Ghosts, time slips, and out-of-body experiences among them.

The first time I meditated was during my forties, and this led me to a significant spiritual awakening. The whole experience changed my view of life and allowed me to live a more meaningful existence.

I wonder if the unusual events I experienced throughout my life were indicators of my growing spiritual awareness.

The second part of my book includes essays I wrote based on my observations and experiences over the years, each reflecting my own personal viewpoint and thoughts about the spiritual realm.

As we are all aware, each individual has a unique perspective on the spiritual world, and yours may differ from mine, but I believe those who have chosen a particular path will understand what I mean.

Most of these stories have been published in my other book, *Night Visions*, so I have only selected those relevant to what I wish to say.

The third part of the book deals with meditations.

## *Changes*

And I have felt
A presence that disturbs me with the joy
Of elevated thoughts; a sense sublime
Of something far more deeply interfused,
Whose dwelling is the light of setting suns,
And the round ocean and the living air,
And the blue sky, and in the mind of man.
A motion and a spirit that impels
All thinking things, all objects of all thought,
And rolls through all things...
[Composed by Thomas Aquinas,]

## *Confusion*

When I was a child, many things other children understood easily were strange to me, and I was a slow learner.

I taught myself to read and write, but arithmetic and other things were impossible to grasp. It took me years to understand basic concepts about life and learning was a nightmare.

During my childhood, my mother had to go away because she was ill. This affected me badly as I did not know where she went. So, a few of my aunties had to take care of me.

In some ways, I felt like a discarded toy instead of a little girl, and it felt as though I had been forgotten by the only person I loved.

Even though I had good cousins, it was their world, not mine.

A leg without its foot is a good analogy.

This left me confused, and I didn't fit in no matter what I did. As a result, I retreated into a world of my own.

Over this time, I was moved from one school to another, which left me with no time to learn the essentials of life, assuming I understood them anyway.

When in the company of my peers, I was at a loss to understand what I was supposed to do, or even how to behave, and even though there were people around me, I often felt alone.

During my stay in a convalescent home recovering from anaemia, I wanted to write a letter to my mother, but was not sure how. Realising this, the nuns put me into a small classroom to catch up with my learning.

The teacher didn't believe I was having trouble, and thought I was faking. To make an example of me, she called me a dunce and sent me to the corner of the room with my back to the children. This caused the other children to make fun of me and call me names.

Nobody tried to understand my odd behaviour, instead they treated me as an object for ridicule. In response to this, I withdrew even more into myself.

If another child approached me, I never knew what to say or do, and children's games such as hopscotch were too confusing. To others, this looked as though I was stupid, but I wasn't.

There was no way to escape my silent world because I didn't know how.

Thinking back on this period of my life I now realise I was different. Ghosts and other supernatural phenomena still scared me, but I thought the world was supposed to be this way, so I never questioned it.

When I was still an infant, I met the ghostly occupant of a house in Cheshire, England.

## *Poppy*

Following the war, my mother worked as a housekeeper in Cheshire, England. She probably wanted to be near my brother, who attended a nearby boarding school.

Her leaving London is a mystery to me, but I think my first father was to blame for her departure.

*An Open Door*

I was only 6 months when we moved into the house, and we had our own room in the attic, but I was far too young to remember much.

As I grew older, my mother took me with her while she cleaned the house.

There was a large room on the ground floor, which had windows on three sides, and doors leading out onto a patio or garden, and as it was pretty, I loved going there.

The room was occupied by a lovely lady who had long, fair hair, pale skin, and dark eyes. She must have been sick, as she was always in bed.

A small table beside the bed held flasks of water and dark brown bottles of liquid. And since I was always ill, I knew they were medicines.

The lady looked as though she had been reading, for on the bed as though she had just that minute laid it down would be a faded leather book.

As I was so young, I didn't ask my mother why she never looked at the lady in bed. Instead, she would dust and vacuum the floor without even glancing at the bed.

The room was filled with poppies. They were on the window ledges, beside the bed, and even on the bed. They never grew old, and always looked vibrant and alive, as if they were just picked.

I felt as though this lovely person liked me, so even if we didn't speak, I would sit happily on the bed with her while my mother dusted.

When I was nine, I asked my mother about the lady in the bed at Miss Lamb's house, and why there had been so many poppies in her room. She looked at me with a look of fear on her face.

"But Grace, there was no one in the room, and no poppies. You must have seen a ghost."

Well, if this was her ghost, why was she so real!

It turned out later that Poppy was Ms Lamb's sister, and she had died in that room.

I now realise that seeing and hearing ghosts was a natural part of my life, and the lady in the bed was just one of many experiences I had as a child.

## *The Ward*

This happened when I stayed in a hospital in London. After having a smallpox vaccination when I was about seven, I experienced dreadful nosebleeds.

Because of losing so much blood, I became anaemic and had to be hospitalised.

There must have been other patients in the ward, but I don't remember them. The only people I remember were the sister who sat at her desk near the door, and the nurses who walked about silently in their big white headdresses and uniforms.

It was a spooky place, as the high ceilings and the eerie atmosphere made it feel cold and impersonal.

Plus, it was unnaturally cold in the ward, an all-pervading cold, which seemed to come from bizarre places such as cupboards, bedpans, or the corners of the room.

While it was daytime, things did not seem too bad, but at night weird shadows drifted across the room, making the curtains and my heart flutter with fear.

The urge to scream was overwhelming, but my vocal cords were frozen, and no sound came out of my mouth.

Then one night, I witnessed shadowy figures walking around the ward. They looked very lost and unhappy, and disappeared into thin air when I made a noise. Although I wasn't sure if they were ghosts, I was terrified, so I hid under the covers and screamed for the nurse.

I am sure I must have scared the whole hospital with my pitiful wails. When I told the nurses about the ghosts, they didn't believe me, but I was convinced of what I saw to this day. I might have seen the spirits of patients who had died.

## *Strange Child*

There was another odd experience I had while I was staying in a convalescent home.

The illness that had landed me in hospital left me so weak, I couldn't walk down the street without becoming breathless and shaky.

A specialist ran some tests on me and confirmed that anaemia (a severe iron deficiency) was the culprit.

My mother was advised to send me to a convalescent home on Hayling Island, which was on the South coast of England, as it had a good reputation for the clean sea air, which the specialist thought would help me.

My mother was assured that I would get better much faster than at home.

I didn't want to leave her because I thought I would never see her again, but with gentle persuasion and a promise that she would visit me, I was reassured.

Ironically, the place where we had to wait for the bus was my favourite park.

All the children travelling on the bus had been sick as well, so I was in good company. Most of us were thin and had pasty complexions, so we all needed the good clean air of the health centre.

As we left, I could see my mother crying, but I tried not to cry, as she had promised I was only going to be away for a few weeks. Little did we know it would be a whole year.

After what seemed hours, we came to a long bridge, which fascinated me, and the light of the setting sun reflecting on the sea brought a lump to my throat. It was easy to imagine walking on Brighton beach with my mother, throwing handfuls of bread at the seabirds and singing with happiness, and I wished she were with me.

As soon as we arrived, we were met by two nuns, and taken into a big room to have some tea. No one understood what was happening, and by then, most of us were too tired to care.

We were given a light tea, but I don't remember what it was now. Then we were taken into a bathroom with heaps of sinks and toilets in, and to a small child it was cold and scary.

The nun told us to wash our face and hands and then follow her.

We were taken to a room with lots of beds beside each other. The only other time I had been in the company of so many children was when I was at school. However, this time I had to sleep in the same room with them as well, so I felt nervous.

All that had happened so far had been unpleasant, and I wanted to go home. What made it harder for me was sharing a big room with crying children. In the end, I pretended to cry too. The false tears turned into the real ones, and soon I was weeping with the rest of them.

Sometimes, my mother would send me sweets and comics, but the nuns disapproved of the practice. However, they were kind enough to read my mother's letters to me, which I appreciated, and they always let me keep the comics.

Children's diseases were endemic, and I was at a disadvantage because of my anaemia. This meant if a child caught a disease, so did I.

My body temperature would soar whenever I contracted a childhood disease, so the nuns bathed me in lukewarm water to decrease it.

These lovely women devoted much time to my care, and I can be thankful they did, or I would never have made it.

Then, mumps got out of control amongst the children, so as an extra precaution the nuns put me into an isolation room.

The isolation room was a stone-building with three or four rooms in it, and it sat directly in the middle of the complex. This meant that anyone looking out of a window could see my building, standing on its own.

The only person I saw was the nun who gave me my meals and checked on my health. Even though she was a sweet person, she often left me alone in my room and I would cry with loneliness.

The loneliness did not last long, as a small boy began visiting me, and each time he arrived he would have comics tucked under his arm for me to read. He was always happy, vibrant, and bouncing with energy.

We played games together and could talk about anything, so I never felt lonely while he was around, and I never wondered how he got there, as I was just happy to have someone to play with.

When I told the nun about him, she was surprised and said I must have dreamt about him, as he wasn't well enough to get up.

After hearing such dreadful news, I insisted on seeing him, so she took me into a room I had never been in before. Then she said sadly.

"Here is your little friend."

The little boy I played with daily was lying on a big hospital bed as though dead. His eyes were closed, and his skin looked so transparent, I could see the veins beneath.

There were tubes and machines going off him in various directions, so it would have been impossible for him to get out of bed.

I was devastated and must have made an involuntary noise, because for a fleeting moment those lovely brown eyes opened, and he looked at me, giving me a feeble smile of acknowledgment. Then he lifted his hand in my direction and gave a very weak wave.

The boy lying on the bed in front of me was nothing like the happy individual who visited me daily, with comics and laughter. Yet, I knew his face and eyes and his tiny thin arms, as though I had known him all my life. Believe me, I was shocked and just could not understand how he could visit me with that thing on his arm?

I don't know what happened to him, but I believe he must have either been moved to a hospital or he had died, because I never saw him after I had been shown his true state of health.

## Angels

Angels is my most published work, and it was an experience that I will never forget, and the reason I am still here talking to you today.

I grew up in England, and when this event happened, only a few houses had bathrooms. To counter this, my mother took me to the bathhouse.

Bathhouses were places where the poorer people of society could pay a small fee for use of a public bath.

The building was huge, with high arches and strange statues throughout, which looked grand to a small child. Inside were many small cubicles, which contained separate baths and showers.

There was also an indoor swimming pool where all the local people could go for a swim, and it was in this pool that I should have drowned.

My mother would leave me sitting beside the child's wading pool to wait for her while she went for a bath. She must have assumed that this shallow bowl of water would keep me entertained.

Upon reflection, she must have thought I was responsible enough to be left alone, and I guess I was, but this time was different.

In awe, I often watched what people were doing in the big pool. They would spring gracefully off the diving board, soaring through the air like birds, before curving into the water. As I watched them, I imagined how it would feel, so I was eager to undertake this magical flight myself.

One day, I realised the big pool was empty. Feeling elated at the thought of trying this beautiful manoeuvre without other people watching, I made my way to the deep end of the pool. Let me tell you now, I did not realise that I had to learn to swim first, for in my innocence I thought everyone could swim.

Innocent and full of courage, I walked toward the big diving board; the only sound was the soft padding of my feet, which echoed around the walls. Then, remembering the diver's graceful moves, I ran to the end of the board and dived in.

Suddenly, the lovely dive I had carried out with precise grace and flair was a thing of the past, and I was terrified when water gushed into my nose and mouth, and I sank below the surface!

As the buoyancy of the water returned me to the surface, I realised with a shock that I could not swim. What made it worse was that I had been stupid enough to wait until everyone had left the pool before diving in. I did not know how to get out of my deadly predicament, so I panicked.

While these terrifying thoughts whirled through my head, I could feel the water drawing me down into its depths. I struggled up to the surface again and gurgled in one last desperate wail.

"Help me."

It was at that moment I saw someone squatting down at the side of the pool. Bending close to the edge, he called out to me, saying.

"Little girl, little girl, please don't panic, just come to me. Move your arms and legs up and down like this," and he paddled his arms and hands in the air in demonstration.

As inexplicable as this may seem now, his soft voice calmed me down enough to stop my panicking, and I obeyed him by moving my arms up and down like he was busy showing me. Somehow, I was no longer afraid that I would return beneath the water. All I felt within me was a calm, peaceful feeling.

The movements he showed me got me back to the side of the pool. Then the gentle stranger pulled me out of the watery hell.

Shaking badly, I looked back at the pool, realising just how silly I had been. Relief spread through me, and I turned around to thank the man for saving me. But he had completely disappeared. It had only been a few seconds since I had been pulled out of the water, but there was no sign of him.

As there were only windows alongside the pool, how had he exited? The only sign that remained was the towel he had flung around my shoulders. Yet without his gentle voice to calm me, I could never have returned to the edge of the pool safely.

Looking back on this incident now gives me a sense of wonder. It does not seem possible that I could have escaped from drowning after my headlong dive, and that my protector had vanished into thin air.

I feel that whoever helped me was from another sphere of existence. Is this the place where angels or guardians live, and maybe they wait to help us when we are in difficulty? I think that just for a moment, my guardian angel was there for me. It had not been my time to go.

∞

There are certainly guides or angels around us, however I call them helpers, and they are there to assist us.

If they appear in your life, send love to them. I am not sure if a guide is in my life or not, however I have seen a strange half girl/boy in my meditations, of course it could have been my imagination also.

Most helpers will give information if you request it, or they will assist you by whatever means is in their power but remember the only way they can help you is when they come directly into your world. Many appear in an emergency, or when your life might be in danger.

## *The Haunting of River House*

River House was the last place I lived in as a child, and it remains one of my happiest memories. One day I would like to visit the river again, even though the house no longer stands.

I was about nine years old when we moved into river house, and it was a wonderful, exciting, and creepy place. It seems like I lived there for a long time, but in fact it was only four short years of my life.

In front of the house was a river, with a little footbridge going across it. This delighted me, and I would spend many hours lying on that tiny bridge, watching the fish swimming happily about in the water. Or I would become interested in the many insects and lizards that gathered on the riverbank. Then, at other times, I would just sit there watching the various birds going about their business.

Unfortunately, the house was haunted, and this tale is about some of my experiences while living there.

The bedroom was in the attic, and it was a good room for me, as it had its own fireplace and a huge built-in wardrobe.

Realising that I had never had a room of my own before, my mother decorated it with pretty furniture and matching curtains. But what made it special was the view out of the window where I could see the small bridge and river.

However, river house was haunted, and my bedroom was the place the ghost liked to visit.

Sleeping in my beautiful bedroom was a luxury I had never experienced before, but this didn't last for long, as I heard someone or something breathing heavily. It was so spooky that I hid under the bedclothes, and yelled for my mother, but as soon as I screamed it stopped, so when she came into the room, there was no more noise. She must have thought it was my imagination.

The next time it happened, it was close to my head, and this time, I ran out of the room in fright. Standing on the landing, I called out to my mother, and she sat with me while we waited for the breathing to start again, but nothing happened. Her solution for everything was prayer, so we prayed.

Thankfully, whatever time of the night it was, she would be there just to keep me company. (A small note here. Even now I wake myself up calling out mummy, how embarrassing.)

Some nights if I couldn't sleep, my mother would tell me long fascinating fairy tales. She made these stories up while she was sitting with me. It's possible her stories encouraged my creativity as I now write children's books.

My father, always the sceptic, insisted it was my imagination, so I wasn't allowed to move to another room. This is when I decided that if I couldn't change my room, then my dog should keep me company.

My father protested, as dogs in bedrooms were unhygienic, but with my mother's help, I smuggled Winker upstairs each night as regular as clockwork. This did the trick, and the nightly visits stopped.

Winker had a mane of soft yellow hair, which made him look like a lion. I loved that dog, and when I was feeling miserable or extra low, I imagined him turning into a handsome prince.

He enjoyed lying on my bed at night, and for a short while it was fine, but he grew into a large dog. In the end, he was demoted to the floor. Or he would have smothered me with his weight.

The ghost, peeved over my pet's intrusion, soon found other ways to scare us, because one day another creepy thing occurred.

My friend and I had just arrived home from school, and we were happily sitting at the table, everybody's favourite place to hang out. The table stood beside the door leading to the staircase...

We were eating jam sandwiches and reading our favourite comics when we suddenly heard someone walking down the stairs. This was just not possible, as we had already been upstairs to change out of our school clothes, and we knew nobody was up there.

We froze and looked at each other in fear. Winker, my dog, looked up at the door and whimpered. Then he took off as fast as his fat legs would carry him, and I can assure you we were not far behind. In a blind panic, we raced into the lounge room and hid behind the sofa.

The ghost continued walking down the stairs, and we heard the staircase door opening. It was easy to imagine the spirit walking into the room we were hiding, so we both hugged Winker close.

As we huddled there, we could hear it walk across the floor and open the front door, which slammed behind it.

Putting on a brave doggy face, Winker found the courage to venture out of our hiding place. We could hear his paws tapping suspiciously over the floor as he went to investigate, and we giggled with relief when we heard his doggy nose snorting and snuffling around the front door. He then trotted back into the room where we were hidden, wagging his tail, and pressing his nose into our hiding place...

My mother also had a rather awful experience in the house a few weeks later, although I am not sure if this can be called supernatural.

Each night for a couple of months, she would dream that she was at the top of the stairs, but instead of walking she would float down in slow motion. These dreams seemed so real that they worried her.

One night her dream became a reality, and the sound of a loud crash and a heart-rending scream woke us all up. We rushed out to see what had happened, only to see poor mother lying at the bottom of the staircase. She had been dreaming again, and this time she had acted it out physically! Thankfully, although she was badly bruised, she did not receive any injuries.

My father just did not believe in ghosts or the supernatural at all. When strange things happened in our house, he thought it was just our imagination, but I think he had underestimated the resident ghost.

One day I was talking to my mother about the ghost, when my father laughed and told me it was all in my imagination. Annoyed, I tried to explain that it was not my imagination and that strange things happened in our house, but I was getting nowhere. Then, to our amazement, a hairbrush that had been lying on top of the piano lifted of its own accord and floated in the air right in front of my father's stunned face. It hovered there for at least twenty seconds before collapsing to the floor.

I can still remember the look on his face to this day, and I will treasure that moment for as long as I live.

Unfortunately, the house where all these adventures happened has long gone, taking its ghost and all. The only thing left standing now is an ornate iron gate.

# Grandfather

Looking back in foresight, I think that if I had a chance, I would have enjoyed both of my grandparents. Sadly, I never spent much time with them.

My grandmother died of heart failure while I was still young, so I don't have many recollections of her, but my grandfather fascinated me.

My grandfather was a cobbler by trade, and when I was young, I would watch him work in awe, and would pretend he was a magician.

Even though I loved him dearly, I had little to do with him, but I am not sure why. However, I believe the mutual feeling between us was there right until the end of his life because many years later when he was dying; he paid me a visit.

When I was about twelve, my mother was called away to be with my grandfather, who was on his deathbed. She left me to look after the house and feed my brother and father, and I know I made a mess of each meal.

One night, about two in the morning, something woke me up. There was a strange, unnatural silence, and everything around me was eerily quiet. It was then I noticed a round light about a foot in diameter; enter the room through the window. Hovering about three feet in the air, the ball of light gradually circled the room, as though looking for something or someone. This terrified me so much that I hid beneath the covers.

Through a tiny crack in the blanket, I watched a ball of light move eerily around my bedroom. Finally, whatever it was, disappeared into the wall, and I emerged from beneath my bedclothes. I found out later this was the moment he died.

∞

Although the next story doesn't have spirits or other things in it, it was a strange experience, and it goes along with other weird happenings in my life.

## *Other Realities*

When this incident occurred, my husband's family was caring for our children while we both worked. And as they lived some miles away from where we were living, we often travelled between towns to visit them.

I had a beautiful voice when I was young, so my mother wanted to hear me sing at her church. This meant I had to sing for the congregation each Sunday, but I longed to stop as I was often too tired. I pleaded with her, but I couldn't get out of it.

On our way home, we had to cover some very lonely roads. One night, we were on our way home after a long day, visiting our children and going to church.

The motorbike, which was only a fifty-cc Suzuki, was struggling under our combined weight, and it sometimes made strange noises as if telling us to stop before it stopped.

However, it was impossible to interrupt our journey, for it would be eleven when we reached home, and we both had to rise at dawn for work.

We were driving home along a dark and deserted back road, and we were both exhausted from the events of the day. All we wished to do was to go home and fall into bed. Yet, as we progressed along the road, of which we had travelled many times before, the landscape took on a strange luminous appearance.

It felt as though we were driving through a long silent tunnel, and on either side of us, the countryside we were so familiar with was disappearing, as though it was being rubbed out as we progressed.

Added to this eerie atmosphere was the lack of the normal night noises. In fact, there were no sounds penetrating this strange zone at all! There was not a single breath of wind or anything living to show that we were still alive.

For a time, it felt as though we were just progressing in a sphere of continuous darkness. The road had ceased to exist, and we were in a strange void, yet we could not stop. It was as if we were being guided forever onward into a world of complete oblivion.

This sensation lasted for what seemed like endless light years of time. Then, as suddenly as it had begun, it dissipated in a flash.

My husband stopped the motorbike, and we clung to each other in fear. What was it? What had happened to us? We only knew we were free from that engulfing black web of terror.

When we arrived home, we were dismayed to realise that some considerable time had elapsed. We had left at ten o'clock and it was now two am. The ride would normally take only about half an hour to an hour, but this time it had taken four hours!

Had we entered a world or area between reality and if this strangeness had continued, would our bodies have been found dead on the side of the road, or would we just have disappeared from this earthly existence?

This wasn't the last experience we had together, but I shall omit them here and continue onto a weird dream I had only a short time after arriving in Australia.

## Strange Dream

Everyone I have told this to believe I had a dream. I won't deny that, but at the time it felt very real.

We were living in a bush house in a remote area of Australia.

One night I was woken up from a deep sleep by a strange light filtering in through the bedroom window. I assumed that someone with a torch was walking about outside, and I wondered why anyone would shine a light so close to our bedroom window. I shook my husband to wake him up, but he only groaned and turned over.

Never one to be daunted by strange things I got out of bed and walked out into the lounge room. Not sure of what to expect, I quietly opened the front door.

What confronted me was so impossible that I had to rub my eyes in disbelief, but the spectacle remained.

Standing on my front lawn was a tiny UFO! It had the obvious saucer shape, but it was not much bigger than a small car. There were high blue windows around the roof, and the craft had a soft silver haze surrounding it. I rubbed my eyes, thinking that I was having a fantastic dream, but if it was a dream, it didn't work as the craft remained.

Two tall, dark-haired males dressed entirely in black were standing beside the steps of the vehicle. They had strange staring eyes and skin so white it glowed in the reflected light of the craft. I am sure that seeing such extraordinary individuals should have frightened me, but this was not the case.

They gestured with their hands, and I realised they wanted me to enter their ship. Then, as though mesmerised, I entered their machine.

As soon as I was inside, we took off at great speed, and although I felt nervous, these two odd beings assured me I was safe by smiling at me and making gestures of friendship.

The craft was ultra-modern, with strange dials, panels, and screens everywhere. The seats were moulded into the craft, and they looked uncomfortable, but when they invited me to sit down, I realised they were soft.

Fascinated, I could see where we were going from the viewing windows, and I realised I was looking into space. In shock, I realised the blue disc we were rapidly receding from was the earth itself.

Viewing the planet in such a manner was an unforgettable experience, and I watched it disappear into the darkness like a jewel.

I was journeying further and further away, but I wasn't afraid. Instead, it felt as though the experience was familiar to me, as though I had undertaken this trip a thousand times.

Below me I could see a silent planet, and the tall men led me to believe this place was part of the moon.

Soon we descended, and as I looked, I realised we were entering a crater of a large, extinct volcano. Above us, I could see a glass-like cover, which was gradually closing as we descended.

We entered a station or landing port where there were other vehicles and many people milling about. I felt like a celebratory because everybody looked eager to see me. It must have been a reception committee as they guided me through a passage into a huge room.

Everyone was wearing tight uniforms of soft grey, and looked nothing like the pilots who had brought me in. Instead, they had fair skin and almost white hair, and their eyes were a vivid blue. They spoke in high childlike voices, but I could not understand a word they were saying.

The situation made me feel panicky and hot and I could not breathe properly. Gasping, I asked a bystander for a glass of water. Their eyes widened in alarm, and they began talking excitedly together.

They must have sent me home, because the next thing I remember was waking up in my bed, with no recollection of the return journey at all!

I was still thinking about the *dream* when I woke up. It had been so real I was determined to write it down before I forgot. As I walked into the lounge area, my gaze went toward the front door, and I received a mild shock because the floor had muddy footprints all over it. I looked down at my feet and realised they were dirty, and there were footprints from the front door to the bedroom!

Could it have been a real experience, after all?

## *An Answer to Prayer*

An Answer to prayer was a miracle for my hungry children, and I am sure they can still remember this incident. Although we had nothing to do with our neighbours, they must have known we were doing it tough.

We were living on a farm property with our young family and completely isolated from civilisation, and as we lived so far from town, the children had to have correspondence school.

We were so poor I had to make bread for their evening meal, and for a time all we survived on was bread and vegemite sandwiches.

One day, feeling thoroughly disheartened with our lot I remembered all the magical things that had happened to us when I was growing up. These miracles often happened after my mother had prayed for help. So, feeling hopeful I told my children about their grandmother's belief in prayer.

After telling the children about the miracles, I suggested we should ask God to send us some food, so we knelt together and prayed that we would have something for tea.

Shortly after our fervent prayers, I was busy in the laundry doing the family wash. I had to wash the clothes in an old-fashioned boiler and did not have a smidgen of washing powder. I felt depressed at the time and needed a miracle just to lift my feelings of despair.

Then I heard the children yelling happily.

One of my children yelled out.

"Mummy, mummy come quickly and see what we have found."

I ran outside thinking they may have found a sick animal, which they were fond of doing, but to my surprise, they were holding heaps of mushrooms in their hands!

Relief flooded through me as now we could eat something different at teatime.

They were bubbling with happiness and told me the mushrooms covered the back paddock, from one fence to the other. And as this was a rather hot part of South Australia, the whole thing was amazing!

Then, just when I had sent them back with a bucket to gather some more mushrooms, one of the farm workers arrived in his truck.

"Here missus, he said, the boss reckons you could use this, hey!"

Then, from the back of his truck, he pulled out a side of lamb, already trimmed and tidied up ready for cooking.

I was so relieved, for now the children could eat reasonably well until our next payday, but that was not all! For later in the day, when my husband came home from work, he had a box in his arms full of Jams and Marmalades. He had found them sitting on a post at the entrance to the driveway.

Someone must have known of our predicament and helped us out without revealing themselves.

Miracles can happen, especially if you believe!

## *Mother's Bibles*

My mother tried hard to find the right church to worship in, and over the years she gathered a large collection of bibles, and these became significant when she died.

My two small sons were now living with my ex-husband in Darwin, and I lived alone in a small apartment in Hawthorn, Victoria.

One morning I was surprised to find mail addressed to me in my father's handwriting.

My father never wrote letters, so this communication caught my attention right away.

In the letter, he told me my mother was in hospital after suffering a heart attack.

It was not possible to fly home to England as I did not have enough money, so to hear this news was traumatic, and I could do nothing except wait and pray.

After replying to my father's letter, I went through the day in a haze of agony of spirit. I couldn't imagine my mother lying helpless in a hospital bed with the strong possibility that she would die.

My mother had always been tough and had pulled through everything life had tossed at her, and now she could die. I was devastated.

### *An Open Door*

In the early hours of the morning, I had a strong dream about my mother. She looked happy and better than I had ever seen her before, and it looked as though she had shaken off forty years.

As she walked toward me, I realised she was holding her bible collection, and a pair of shoes. Then, without a word, she handed me her bibles, and the shoes.

Accepting her bibles but puzzled about the footwear, I asked her why I needed shoes and what use could they be to me?

"Grace, she said walk a mile in my shoes. Then, as she turned away from me. She waved and said, I am going now, bye-bye."

I didn't know what she meant, and I must have looked confused, but instead of a response she walked away with a smile on her face.

When I woke up, I realised my mother had just visited me, and although it was only a dream, it had been very real.

Not long after waking, a telegram arrived from my father to say that my mother had died in her sleep. I am sure that if my mother had not taken the time to visit me when she left, the blow would have been harder for me to bear.

It took a long time for me to accept that my mother had passed *over* and many years before real tears were released.

Over the years, I have pondered on her words, and I think I now know what she was trying to say. The words *walk a mile in my shoes*, intended to imply that I should help others as she had done throughout her life. Her strength of character helped members of her close family, friends, and complete strangers go through rough patches in their lives. She gave her love and support willingly to all who needed it, including visiting dying people in hospital.

I have always looked at my mother as a saint because of the love she gave willingly to others. Let us all walk a mile in her shoes.

The departed don't always appear as ghosts. Some appear in our dreams, too. After my mother left, I sometimes saw her in dreams, and over the years she would visit me to warn me of things.

The last time she visited she was holding a purse and walking upstairs. She looked back at me, smiled, and waved as though she was going on a long journey.

## In the Corner

The first time an out-of-body episode happened to me I was when I was in my late twenties and a full-time mother of five children.

Poor health plagued me, and I almost left my family motherless a few times because of asthma and pneumonia.

When we first arrived in Australia in 1966, we lived in South Australia, and for a few years all was fine, but it soon became clear finding work other than timber cutting was difficult for my hubby.

Finally, he found work with my uncle Fred in Victoria, so we moved. However, my health did not improve in fact it got worse.

Not long after we had moved, I became extremely ill with pneumonia, and as we could not afford a hospital visit; the Doctor came to the house. Since she understood our financial problems, she never asked for money.

As I was so sick, she had to give me injections every half-hour. These medications helped my breathing. However, I had just finished having one of these shots when my heart began pounding, and for a flash, a fraction of a second, I jumped out of my physical body.

A moment later, I found myself up near the ceiling, looking down at my husband and doctor, who were in a state of frantic concern.

Although this incident was only for a second, it was all I needed to understand that I was conscious outside of my body.

## *Walking Outside*

Walking outside was another out-of-body experience I had when I was living in Darwin

Have you ever had a dream that was more than a dream, where it felt as if you were outside of your body, and everything you witnessed during this time was as real as if you were awake, I have?

One night a strange feeling woke me up. It felt as though my body was vibrating rapidly and my heart was pounding. It was so scary I thought I was having a heart attack. What made it even more frightening was that I could not move a muscle, and the only noise I could make was a strange guttural sound at the back of my throat. If I were having a heart attack or stroke, no one would know, so I was terrified!

Suddenly, I was standing beside my bed. Strange as it may seem now, it didn't bother me. I knew that if I were to look at my body, it would still be there, either asleep or dead.

This thought made me nervous, so I was too scared to look at myself. Instead, I walked out of my bedroom door and into the kitchen. I can remember the colours looked alive.

I wondered if I should go into my friend's bedroom, but she might think I was a ghost, and this would scare her out of her wits. Dismissing this idea, I thought I should go outside, but when I looked at the front door, I realised it was locked.

It was then I recollected hearing about astral travel. Apparently, in that bodiless stated we could walk through walls and doors, and that is what I did.

What an experience! It is difficult to explain the feeling. The only way to describe it is when someone has taken mind-altering drugs, as their mind does the most unusual things, and their perception is transformed.

When I put my hand out to touch the door, I could feel a tingle, like mild static electricity. I eased forward, and as I did so, I could feel the wood stretching around me. Then suddenly, I was on the other side of the door.

I was surprised to find that it was as light as day outside, but this did not bother me for long, as I was too interested in everything around me. I looked up into the sky, wondering if I could fly, and just as if my thoughts could move me, I drifted upwards.

As I floated into the sky, I had a sudden thought.

"What if I am dead and I am going somewhere else?"

In my panic, I tried to control the upward drift, but I realised I had no control of my actions at all! I am sorry to declare that floating away on the breeze or whatever, with no control of my own, frightened me so much that I came back into my physical body with a mighty thump!

Waking up alive in my body and awed by the whole episode, I realised that if there had been no fear of dying, I could have travelled anywhere.

These out-of-body experiences have convinced me we don't die, but just take on another form.

Unusual experiences such as these may have been indicators of my growing spiritual awareness, or perhaps this ability was present from the beginning, unrecognised until later in life.

I have experienced subtle shifts in consciousness throughout my life, but they were not fully understood until I meditated for the first time.

It is worth noting here these changes in my consciousness seem to happen over ten-year intervals, but I did not realise this until I began meditation.

By 1988, I had experienced many disruptions in my life, like moving home and the break-up of a relationship.

Then, to top it off, I was diagnosed with a prolapsed uterus, which had to be removed.

There was a moment where I died on the table, but nobody in the hospital admitted this, and I only learned about it after the doctor found a spot on my chest where adrenalin had been injected.

When I moved into a tiny one-bedroom unit to live on my own, I realised I enjoyed being alone.

In 1989, a demanding job had caused me to suffer, and I developed a strange headache that I could not get rid of.

The only thing, which might have caused the pain was an accident I had when I fell off a swinging exercise machine and hit the top of my head. Yet, the pain or pressure was not at the top of my head, but between my eyes, so to ease the headache, I tried meditation.

My first meditation was a revelation. It lasted 20 minutes, and when I opened my eyes, the world around me looked different. Everything was alive. Outside, the trees, grass, and the air shimmered with a deep concentrated light.

The more I practiced, the more I realised there was a silent communication with nature and unity with everything.

The headache had gone as though it was never there, and everything felt peaceful. Even my dreams were realistic and were more like visions instead.

Something had changed within me, and I saw things in a new light. My mind was clear, and amazing as it sounds now, I understood many things, which I hadn't before.

Every time I meditated it felt as though I was opening a door to another way of thinking, or another dimension of reality.

Shortly after this, a wonderful experience happened, and I had to write it down, as it was unreal.

Here is an account of the life-changing events, which happened to me over a few months.

## *Realities Edge*

In 1989, I was living alone in an old pre-cyclone one-bed roomed unit in Darwin, and I was training to be a florist in a little shop in town. However, I had a lot of trouble with the manageress, as she hated the attention the owner gave to me. Twice out of sheer desperation, I had walked out of the shop never to return. But the owner, a sweet elderly gentleman talked to her and calm things over, so back I came

For a while, things were ok, and I happily cleaned the flower room or answered the phone. I had been employed as a trainee florist to learn the Art of flower arrangement, but the manageress refused to teach me. Instead, she was very demanding and imposed severe pressure on me, which did nothing to help me learn, as I am useless under pressure and will make mistakes I don't normally make.

As part of my everyday life, I attended a healing course and developed an interest in spirituality. One day I came across a numerology book at the library. This was something I could understand, and it was not long before I started doing readings for others.

Numerology works with numbers and how they influence one's life, and it should have been straightforward. However, I couldn't understand why I sensed things about the person I was reading for.

During one reading I felt extremely hot, not sure what to say I said,

"I can feel intense heat around me."

Unfortunately, my reading caused an uproar, as a few days later their house caught fire and burned to the ground.

Since I was not looking forward to being the bearer of such unfortunate news, I wanted to stop, however my prediction sparked an interest with other members of the same family who begged me for another reading, so I gave in.

This time it felt as if someone around them might die, so as not to cause panic I said.

"There is a sense of loss around you." Two days later, their grandmother died. The events had such an impact on me I stopped doing the readings soon after.

At around this time, several strange events took place, which made no sense, but the most peculiar thing was a pressure directly between my eyebrows. It was strange as it felt as though someone was pressing a thumb against my forehead with all the force they could muster.

This strange feeling increased until I felt I would go crazy. I tried dulling this nagging sensation with various analgesics and other potions, but to no avail. Now I am no firm believer in doctors, but this was intolerable, and I was desperate for an answer. What if I had a brain tumour? But before going to a doctor, I tried other methods.

Meantime back at the shop, I realised I could no longer endure the manageress's spiteful remarks. One day after a gruelling experience, I took off my apron, picked up my bag, and told her where to go, then with a sigh of relief I walked out of the shop forever.

I realised I had to sort out my life, and to release the unbearable pressure in my head, which was there as a constant throb. After wondering if it might be caused by tension, I went to a new age bookshop run by a friend and explained what was happening. He looked puzzled and suggested that I could use the float tank, which may help relax me. Honestly, although he had led the workshop on healing, which I had attended, I don't believe he had the slightest idea of what was wrong with me.

The float tank holds a saline solution, which allows the body to float. According to the theory behind it, if one floated in a warm salt bath, they would feel as if they were back in their mother's womb. This was supposed to bring psychological relief and relax a person.

As I lay there waiting for something to occur, I thought of the wonders of this treatment that other occupants had talked about. A few of them had visions, and several had travelled in a bodiless state to other places.

However, I couldn't understand how anyone could relax lying in water. It may be full of salt so that it was not possible to sink, but it was still water. To compensate, I lay my head to one side, which left me wondering if the water might go into my ears, so I put my head to the other side with the same effect. When nothing happened, I felt disappointed.

Before long, floating in water felt familiar, and I relaxed. It was then I saw three Dolphin swimming toward me. This imagery was fascinating, as it was like a film being projected on the front of my head. I was aware of where I was, yet on another level I was watching my visitors swim and dive on the surface of a vast inland sea.

Unfortunately, my visitors did not come any closer, for at the very moment of their arrival, the time in the tank was over and I had to get out.

After the experience, I received a massage which felt very relaxing and eased some of the tension created by the job I had just left. But I could still feel the pressure in my head, and instead of easing, it had become more intense.

I could not tell De... that his float tank had no desirable effect, as I knew he would not understand, and as he was such a kind-hearted man, I didn't want him to think I was unappreciative.

When I walked to the front of the shop, which held various books on spiritual enlightenment, self-help, gurus, and channels, I felt bewildered.

When I had been a young woman, I had read a book called *The Third Eye*, written by someone calling himself Lobsang Rampa. The book had covered the phenomenon of astral travelling and chakras in some detail. Unfortunately, after the success of his first book, this man's senses appeared to have left him. Because the last two he penned were fabrications of the absurd, and I had put them down in some disgust and proceeded on to subjects with a more logical theme.

I tried to find the original book, but the enormous collection was too much, and I was ready to give up. In fact, I was walking out of the shop when I noticed a title, which stirred my imagination, and I picked up a small paperback book called *The Edge of Reality* by Dawn Hill. As I flicked through the pages, it looked interesting enough to hold my attention. So, thanking my friend I paid him and left, deep in contemplation.

I did not go home immediately, instead I sat down on the beach. I had done this in the past couple of months, especially when confusion and frustration threatened to overwhelm me.

Once more, I was sitting here, but the decision, which had been plaguing me for a while had been resolved, and it was at that moment I felt relief soar through me. I became so engulfed in this emotion that I shouted out.

"Thank you for being there for me."

I had no job, and no prospects of obtaining another, with my lack of work history and age factor, but for the first time in about two-and-a-half years, I felt happy. What strange fate was ahead of me? What was happening? I was to find the next part of my life interesting and magical.

Dawn Hill's book didn't speak about the pressure in my head, but she had a good knowledge of spiritual things and could express them well.

The meditations described in her book covered a larger range than I had encountered before, and I felt that if I practiced this discipline daily, it would improve my life and may even relieve some of my stress.

I had previously learned to meditate but at the time I had not been serious. Thus, I was eager to undertake this discipline again.

I taped one meditation, which allowed me to relax while performing it. It had caught my eye because it was a colour meditation and I like colours.

The colour meditation takes one through the Chakras, and whilst doing this it cleanses and clears away negative energies and thoughts.

I practiced meditation whenever I could, but at first, the pressure in my head remained, but as it was relaxing, I continued.

It takes time to quieten the mind and calm one's thoughts as they wander everywhere on their own tangent. However, soon I began noticing a lovely glow in the front part of my head every time I meditated.

The glow grew in intensity to become a white light, which filled my head, and I would immerse myself in the light for much longer than the original meditation.

When I opened my eyes, everything around me seemed to be alive, and I felt as though I was connected to the universe. Colours were different, and looked vivid, and if I ventured outside, the trees, grass, and even the air would shimmer with a deep concentrated light.

My sense of oneness was higher than anything I'd ever experienced, as though I was connected to everything around me, and even the plants seemed to communicate with me silently.

In my waking and sleeping, I experienced a clear, unfettered view of life. People whom I had known for years seemed to be lit from within and glowed with great inner intensity.

There was a subtle energy surrounding them, and even though I couldn't see it, I felt it radiating from their presence. I was aware of many colours around the person I was talking to, and it fascinated me.

In this state of utter harmony, I could link with universal energy and feel connected with everything.

Even my dreams were now fantastic, and I travelled to unknown places. In the meditations, I had strong dreams or visions, and it felt as though I was experiencing them for real.

The first vision was delightful, but I did not know what it meant, and even now I can only guess at the interpretation. Maybe someone on a higher level may see other meanings in these visions who knows?

In the vision, I was walking along a path surrounded by a lovely rainforest. There were plants with flowers on them filled with pleasing colours, and the forest trees were alive with energy.

Ahead of me, sitting in a clearing was a green stone, (perhaps a Jade). This stone was big and took up the whole of the path ahead of me. It had a huge presence as though it possessed a spirit and life of its own, and it shimmered in all directions, lighting up the forest surrounding it.

I was so fascinated with this lovely stone that at first; I failed to notice the Indians on every side of me.

These lovely beings looked like Amazon Indians, as they were short of stature and had the typical features and dress of this group. They didn't notice me, for they were more interested in the beautiful green stone. It was like nectar to them, and they were kneeling and stroking it with utter abandonment. Although I didn't understand their language, their veneration was obvious. They were worshiping the stone as though it were a god.

It was then I saw myself carrying the stone in my arms and walking away from them into the forest. With that last puzzling action, I came out of my vision.

Green is a wholesome colour and to me it denotes love. Love has the power to create everything good and beautiful in our vast universe, and my journey was toward this goal.

The Indians are part of the rainforest and know all its secrets. They belong to it and love it with a pure, instinctive insight.

For, is this not what we all should do? Acknowledging love and all its vast stores of wisdom?

When I lifted the stone, it felt as if I was acknowledging the love and light granted to me daily, and yet, it was more than that. I recognised the gift of intuition, a gift that elevated the spirits of the forest and flew on wings to heights unknown.

Within my material form lived a magnificent being, and this being was my spirit, and my spirit was accepting intuitive wisdom into my very existence.

With eyes to see and ears to hear, I could hear the universe singing its praises to life itself and see the light within a human soul glistening brightly.

One night while in a deep meditation, I had another intense *vision*. This time I was in a cave deep within a hillside. On the walls, fire torches flickered, lending an eerie glow to the cavern. Whilst on the floor was a fire with stones surrounding it.

Gathered around the fire in a circle were several monks in brown robes. One monk walked towards me, holding an old leather book. When he arrived at my side, he said something like

As he handed me the book he said.

"You must know the truth."

The book was huge, and I had to lay it down on a wooden stand made for the purpose. Its pages were old and yellow. After looking at these stylish handwritten words, I realised they answered questions about life itself, and for a moment, a fraction of a second, I knew everything there was to know.

Awed over this revelation, I longed for this outpouring of enlightenment to continue so I could bring it back to reality. Instead, I found myself back in my tiny flat.

The remarkable knowledge that I had received, dissipated as fast as melting ice. Still, I guess it would have been impossible to keep such knowledge in its entirety, since the mind cannot comprehend such a task.

The pressure, which had been drumming inside my head day and night for weeks, was no more. It had ceased to exist as though it had never been.

In the days that followed this *vision*, I was continually awed over what was occurring within me, as it felt as if I had within my grasp a vast gift. It was as though anything I wished to know was there in my mind as soon as I needed it.

When I tried to write about the thoughts in my head, they raced through my mind at such a speed I couldn't keep them. Then I hit on the idea of taping them instead. Again, it seemed as if I could not say the words fast enough, and they became lost in translation, and sounded strange and jumbled as though I had lost my mind. Yet, this was not true, for there were concepts and ideas I had never understood before.

Despite this, many thoughts and ideas persisted, I experienced a clear, unhindered view of life.

My thinking changed, and it was as if I was learning things I should have known and many things I had always been curious about.

My friends believed I had lost it completely. How could I know things I had never learned? Who had told me these things and who or what was telling me? They were concerned about the sudden change in my personality. For I, who had been one of the boys, was lecturing to them about many things.

These great revelations and concepts came to me daily, and although I didn't know where this knowledge was coming from, I was not afraid, and never lost one friend while all this was happening. On a lighter note, I guess they thought I had just gone *Troppo*, a Darwin malady.

In the period of this event, I penned these words.

From where do these inspirations stem from?

Can they really emerge from an uneducated mind such as mine?

Yet they come, unprovoked and sudden.

This mind has been exposed to a new consciousness.

How is this possible?

Could it be that this knowledge has always been waiting, lying dormant just beyond reach?

Oh, questions that plea for answers.

Is there then a source from where these great inspirations are just biding their time? Waiting for the right time to bring them into being?

Taking form like an artist's painting.

And could this source be the very essence that gave life to man and all existence?

Am I then similar to a sponge absorbing all these inspirations and ideas?

Am I really the same person who was a failure at school and called a dunce, an imbecile, derided and ridiculed?

What has happened to the being that once inhabited this shell?

What miracle has rearranged the neurones within my mind?

Can I really be the same person as I was before?

As you can see by this disclosure, these events overawed me. Indeed, I was not sure if I was myself any longer. I felt an immense energy surge throughout my being, and a wondrous sense of confusion and awe followed me day and night. Yet, this omnipotent power was gentle and benevolent to me.

A clairvoyant read an account of the dream or vision I had after this experience and explained the change in my personality could be the start of my spiritual journey.

Could the graphic descriptions flowing throughout my story describe the level of growth I had reached in this life journey? And as there were many colours described in my story, she thought they could represent the Chakras.

I felt relieved to hear her words because I had been dubious about my sudden inspirations. However, she could not explain what the pressure in my head was, or why I had been overwhelmed with such sudden enlightenment.

## *A Vision*

The story or vision came to me while I slept. Late at night, the words of this unusual narrative, of which had so mystified me, would rush through my head. Here are the words I wrote.

Am I awake, is this reality? If I am awake, then why do the dreams continue inside my head? I can't let them go. It feels as though someone has turned a tap on and left it dripping. I feel an intense urge to write about what I am seeing before it disappears, and I lose it forever.

As I glance at the clock on the dresser, I realise it is two in the morning, yet I am powerless to refuse this task. I would like to remain in bed, but it does not happen. The story is too important, and I must write it down as soon as possible.

Finally, I can take no more, so I put on my dressing gown and go into the kitchen. When I have put the kettle on, I sit down at my typewriter.

Words and pictures are flowing through my mind at a tremendous rate, and I must write.

I am not sure how much time has gone, but I hear hissing, and realise it is coming from the stove. I get up to remove the kettle and burn my fingers while doing so. As I run my hands under the cold water, I wonder what has happened to me.

Sometimes, as I write, there is a sensation that I am not there at all. I can see my fingers typing, but there are no feelings or sensations in my hands or body. Everything feels light and airy, as though I am in two places at the same time.

It feels as though I am still asleep, hovering somewhere above me. At other times, I wake up already dressed, sitting at my typewriter watching my fingers type.

Over the past few weeks, this has been happening every morning. I don't eat, and when I look up, the day has gone. I must stop or I will starve, but it is hard to draw myself away from the typewriter.

This vision flows from my mind to my fingers and transport me to another place.

I am flying above a vast expanse of ocean; below me, I see a circular island. Several small rivers branch off from the centre of the mainland like the rays of the sun.

Huge parklands are everywhere, and several parks have wonderful waterfalls that cascade toward the ground, and as I watch, tiny droplets of water reflected by the sun form rainbows of colour.

The trees are gigantic, and their branches reach for the sky. There are strange birds among the branches. Each bird's plumage is superb and vibrant. There are hues of reds, blues, yellows, and greens, displayed with taste.

Most birds have long, lacy feathers that flow down beneath them, like the bird of paradise. They are divine creatures of light and dreams.

These exquisite creatures are singing magnificent songs, and the music they make is soft and round. It fills the soul, creating a peaceful feeling deep within me.

I fly above buildings, which sparkle in the sun, as though they have crystals embedded within their walls. Fascinated, I allow myself to drift lower to examine them in more detail. Here I find huge marble columns of the finest textures, and each slab of marble fits together so well I cannot see where it begins or ends.

As I drift past, I reach out and touch each building. Their texture is smooth, like glass. Each touch produces a calming energy, which flows through my body, as though the very stone was a living being.

The walls are warm, and vibrate as I touch them, and as I gaze with wonder at the semi-transparent walls, I notice moving shapes within. The shapes are tall beings wearing long robes, yet my eyes cannot focus on them for long and they disappear.

These elusive beings appear unaware I am watching them, and I get the impression they are entities from a higher realm or dimension.

I feel as if I belong here, as though I once lived in this magical place.

A memory is taking shape in my mind, and in it, I am sitting with others on the steps of one of these impressive buildings. We are listening in rapt attention to what tall beings clothed in golden garments are saying. They are holding massive books, but instead of words, the books have pictures. The pictures draw the viewers into the book, as though they are inside the story.

Both the males and females wear delicate gowns, which flow around the figure, and woven in these costumes are dazzling radiant colours, which seemed to dance and move.

To my untrained eyes, it feels as though music and fragrance were intertwined within the material.

There is nothing in this material world that compares to the beauty and magic I experience in this place.

I wonder now is this the place where souls go after they leave this earthly life? Is this another dimension? Maybe it is the long ago past, or could it be a future not yet seen?

## *The Golden City*

Oh, golden city
My home, my love, I have left you
You were home for so long
I loved, I sang, I danced within your walls.
I stepped upon your pyramids and played within your gardens.
I ate the foods of your fields and felt the pain of leaving.
I worshipped the sky gods and watched them destroy you.
I want to return to the place I love, to the place of peace.

Grace Lee

Having reflected on the wonderful vision now, I believe it may have been a powerful method of teaching me inner wisdom. Was it a gentle way of learning, which wouldn't frighten or harm me in any way? Or was the story or vision a catalyst for my increasing spiritual enlightenment?

Do we each have memories of a time when this place existed, hidden deep within our genetic code, spiritual bodies, or both? Maybe the answer to this is yes on all counts.

Was this a glimpse of a divine place our spirits go to, when our earthly life is over, a home where we all belong, and perchance the life we are now living is just an illusion. Alternatively, could it be a place of renewal? Where all knowledge exists.

Or is this a place prophets and others go when they are called to the path of enlightenment? To re-establish the memory of glory and power still in existence in our universe.

After experiencing the vision and having concerns about forgetting the vision, I immediately wrote out my memories, or incidents, so I would not forget them.

As one can see, I have never forgotten. How could I? I will never forget these enriching visions.

They were a gift, a wondrous teaching, which I have been privileged to receive.

In my daily life, I had new vigour and could comprehend concepts that had been out of my reach for most of my life.

As a child, I had been an underachiever, finding school subjects hard to grasp. Now I could go back to college and study everything of which had been a nightmare at school. Subjects so daunting in my school days came to me easily, as though set before me like a delicious meal.

Because of such a life-changing experience, my learning sped up rapidly, and three months later I passed a further education exam.

All this allowed me to apply for a Bachelor of Fine Art degree, at the Northern Territory University.

I feel this potential for further learning may have been lying dormant within me, waiting for a catalyst such as this to shake it from the dark corners of my mind.

Meditation allowed me to access an area of my brain I could not access before. It was as though my brain had been activated from a deep dormant sleep and I could understand many things.

When I meditate, I tap into a consciousness or energy, and I become part of it, yet I must return to the material world, or I would lose my way.

It is the same as when we sleep. In sleep, we are part of consciousness, but our material body is still there waiting for our return.

I believe meditation is a critical practice, because for humanity to recognise itself, it must realise the inner silence within.

It is knowledge of self, which brings awareness. For if we know ourselves, we can recognise each other and the universal consciousness of the entire world. We can then take control of our lives.

When knowledge is given, it opens direct communication to the essence of divinity, which abides within and around us and brings an awareness of everything.

This feeling has never left me; but life must be lived in this reality, and we cannot remain in this state forever.

Of course, I am no intellectual giant or prophet. However, I must state with emphasis, I changed and became an entirely new person. I had more clarity and comprehension, and I looked at life differently.

This experience left me with a deep thirst for knowledge, whether it was maths, literature, philosophy, or art. Learning is something I want to do and will continue to do. Yet, this was just a taste of the exhilarating power which was growing within me. The next stage of this progress would bring even stranger things.

As you have gleaned from the book so far, strange things have happened to me throughout my life, and I have experienced unusual events from a young age. This has made me wonder if some people have more awareness of the spiritual world.

Recently, I was told that I was an *Empath.* At first, I was not sure what this meant until it was explained to me. Whenever I am close to another person, I can sense, see, and hear what is going on inside them on an emotional level. There are no other words to explain this. I just know!

If they are ill or having emotional problems, I sense this and sometimes I can help them.

I believe some people experience more extraordinary incidents than others, but I am not sure why.

I genuinely believe meditation is an important practice. Each one of us needs to know their inner strengths and have knowledge of self, which brings true awareness. For if we can't understand ourselves, how can we understand each other, and the common consciousness of the entire world.

With this knowledge, we can then take control of every part of our lives.

Meditation can benefit a wide range of people. When we reach this state of inner silence, we can remove the blocks in our energy. In doing so, we soon discover that we can transcend mundane worldly thoughts and activities and connect with universal consciousness.

If we are connected to this core of energy, we can reach any place within or around this planet we call home. It would be possible to walk and talk with spiritual beings, and if we needed information, it would be there.

Meditation is not really difficult it just takes letting go of the worldly grind.

## *The Spirit of Man*

I touched the earth and felt its pulse

I tasted the wind on my tongue

I flew above the clouds and saw

The spirit of man

Was really one

I searched within the deepest hollows

Caves deep within the frozen earth

I felt the water on my skin

And realised I have never been

I smelt the stench of poison winds

And heard the groan of many beings

Calling for eternal light

I saw the bodies of many birds

Falling in their daily flight

I cried for all the pain and suffering

And heard the spirit speak to me

*An Open Door*

Why cry when you can never change

Why cry when you can never be

New worlds form by breath of spirit

Old worlds die the same

But man will last forever

He can return again

I heard the fearful wind of fire

Spew forth, devouring all

And deep within its rushing power

The spirit of man stood tall

Grace Lee

## *Alpha Dynamics*

Shortly after this life-changing experience, a friend and I became interested in a course in Alpha Dynamics, as a way of improving our memory.

Although this was a different way of thinking than what we were used to, it can be traced back far into ancient history.

Even though I had learned much from my spiritual experience, I believe the further training in this field gave me a push start into the vast spaces of the mind and spiritual dimensions.

The course was aimed at improving our memories and the methods used were mind expanding, but I am not sure if we all experienced the same thing. Maybe because I had already received such wonderful insights, I gained much from it.

After being made to feel at ease, everyone had to embrace one another with warm, fuzzy hugs. Hugging perfect strangers was weird, as most of us were disconnected from other people. However, it helped us to relax and open up to an interconnectedness we had lost in our mad dash through life.

The first part of this three-day course was to produce relaxation through meditation, which by now I was familiar.

Our teacher described the different levels of sleep, beta, alpha, theta, and delta.

The alpha level was when we were just on the verge of sleep and the best time for relaxation and accessing many things, with memory being just one of them.

We did a meditation of which I was already familiar. It took us through the seven colours, red, orange, yellow, green, blue, violet, and white.

Whilst in this meditative state, we were asked to use our imagination.  The first thing we did was to imagine being inside an apple or a piece of wood, feeling the texture, taste, and smell of these things as though we were part of the object.  The exercise helped us to use our minds differently.

This technique allowed us to experiment like a child, and there were many giggles and much kidding about, and the whole room had a classroom feel to it.

If you think about it, we have a vast symphony of abilities to explore within us.  Maybe by allowing our minds to stretch and expand like little children we are no longer hampered by our pre-conditioned ideas. In this way, we can let them tune into another reality.

We then had to create or imagine a powerful being who was there solely for our own use. Someone who gave us advice and guidance if we needed it.

The lesson had a spiritual element to it, but many of us felt uncomfortable, and trying to imagine an invisible being is hard to do.

However, it was not long before everyone in the room had created someone they could talk to and communicate with, even if it was only through imagination.

There was a lesson called *distant viewing*.

For this procedure, we had to pair up with another person, and give each other a name of someone we knew, and where they lived.

That was all. No other information was divulged. We then had to enter the alpha state and to *see* this person. We had to visualise what they looked like, right down to the last little whisker, and diagnose what was wrong (if anything) with their health, giving remedies, which might help them.

This exercise was successful, and nine out of ten of us had the person's description correct.

Since that time, I have used this successfully when reading for others or trying to understand any specific illnesses they might have.

These exercises allowed me to understand that something other than my imagination is at work within me, and I perceived things with a deeper insight. [v]

## *Growing and Learning*

After all these wonderful experiences, everyday life intruded, and I moved around the country, travelling with a friend. Our primary residence was Cairns, but my friend wanted to live independently, so I had to find a place to live.

My neighbourhood attracted a lot of undesirables, and because of this, I visualised the house I'd like to live in.

I don't have the original request anymore, but here is what I remember.

*The unit must be in a quiet area.*

*It must be spacy and big enough for my art. Hopefully, it would have a bedroom upstairs.*

*A bright kitchen and a front and back porch would be nice, and hopefully it wouldn't be too far from the bus stop.*

There was much more, but it has gone with time. That very night I dreamt of a home with a mezzanine floor, except there seemed to be a railway running along the back hills.

On the following day, I saw a place in Whitfield, and it was exactly what I asked for and dreamed about. It even had a mezzanine floor, which held the bedroom.

On the hill was a small train track that was only used for cane trains, and they didn't operate all the time.

Everything about the unit felt right and even though it was opposite a school; it had a wonderful ambiance to it, so I moved within the week.

## *Parallel Worlds*

Shortly after I moved into the new unit, things began happening to me, which defied any rational explanation, and for a while it felt that I was living in a science fiction story!

My life has always been interrupted by strange events, but this took the cake!

Walking to the shopping centre, close to home, was a pleasant trip, and I often met lovely people on the way who would say hello. One day whilst on the return journey I sensed a presence behind me. Turning around, I saw a young man about three paces away from me. He looked distressed, as his expression was like someone with emotional problems.

He was roughly dressed, and I could see his knees showing through his jeans. Of course, this put me on my guard.

Because I felt self-conscious, I looked away, but looked around again almost immediately to reassure myself he would not attack me. However, to my utter astonishment he had disappeared! There was nowhere he could have vanished in that short time, and I was perplexed. In fact, I even looked behind a bush to see if he was hiding from me, but no, he had gone. It was just not possible for this person to vanish, as the road was wide, and one could see in every direction. This disturbed me, so I hurried home with some haste.

Can you imagine what I felt like? It was an incredible thing that happened to me, and I had to dismiss it as an aberration of my mind or be classified as delusional. In fact, I had all but forgotten the incident until it reoccurred a couple of weeks later. This time, it was an old man who was hobbling toward me, holding a cane for support, and was intent on every step he took as he walked toward me.

My attention was briefly drawn to my feet after I had stepped into some water, and when I looked up again, the old man was gone. There was no way that he could have passed me without me seeing him, and there was nowhere for him to exit.

Again, I went home baffled and confused. What was happening to me and why?

I tried phoning some spiritual people, but instead of giving me helpful advice, they implied that I should have my head examined. They really did not believe me at all. In fact, I think they thought I was having them on. These people were supposed to understand such things!

Several frustrated phone calls later, I finally found someone who believed me.

Indeed, I had to have confirmation that this event was not odd or unusual for my peace of mind, or I would have to believe I was ready for the funny farm.

These strange events did not end with those two occurrences, and I saw a dog who vanished in front of my eyes, and a boy on a pushbike who was there one minute and gone the next.

However, another incident left me completely bewildered, until I understood what was happening to me.

In our city was a small shopping complex, which had escalators leading to a few shops and a post office on the upper floor. At the top of these moving stairs is a kiosk, or I should say used to be a kiosk, selling lottery tickets and such like. I had noticed it as I walked past and thought to myself, I will buy a scratchy ticket when I had done my business at the post office. In fact, I entered two other shops before I made my way back to the kiosk.

After doing all my odd jobs and even looking in the bookshop just beside the kiosk, I turned around intent on buying my ticket, and without too much thought on my mind, I went toward the place where it stood. As I looked up, I realised it was gone. Instead, all that was left were a few markings on the floor where it once had been! How could this be, for I had noticed it several times whilst going backward and forwards in my journey through the shopping complex?

Stunned, I walked back into the bookshop I had just exited and asked the proprietor if the kiosk had been removed in the last half-hour. She looked at me strangely and said in a kind voice.

"Oh no dear, that was moved two weeks ago."

As you can see, I appeared to be living in two worlds. I have become accustomed to these events now, but at the beginning it caused me no end of stress and consternation. Yet, these incidents are as real to me as the physical, and the people I see in them are very material and solid. Indeed, I am sure I could go up to them and touch them and they would respond.

I feel that once one has opened their mind to the possibilities of parallel realities, then they live in a different time zone than other people. It feels like I have opened a door to a different way of looking at life.

Once I was aware of a new reality; and I could never turn back. It was like going to a new land and seeing new scenes and people.

Soon I became conscious of many things I had taken for granted.

I once had a dream where I was travelling in a spaceship, and outside the window, I could see planet earth in all its glory. The vivid blue surrounding our lovely planet amazed me, and a lump rose in my throat, knowing this was my home.

To see the truth was just like this. A whole new dimension opened up to me, and I realised we are not alone in this vast universe.

During that time, I didn't realise I had been given a gift that wasn't yet fully activated. The gift was being able to see, feel, and hear what problems people were suffering from. This included far-sight, which gave me the ability to do readings.

However, what disturbed me was to see the same people returned almost weekly, and I felt they were not looking for readings but for reassurance.

Although it saddened me to stop, I realised I needed to learn more. In the end, I did a counselling course as a way of helping them.

Looking back on this period in my life, I realise I was only at the edge of understanding what was happening.

Even though learning to be a counsellor was important, I was unaware of what was happening to me did not belong in the physical world but was part of my spiritual growth.

In 2001, a young girl mysteriously disappeared, so I meditated in order to find her. In a vision, I found her lying beside a river. She told me she had been murdered. She then showed me a man with a dark complexion.

The police found her body beside a river and there was a suspect, but as he was a police officer, he got away with it. But I am sure he murdered her.

During this time, I was in contact with a dowser, a person who uses dowsing rods to locate objects. We went out to search the rivers, and I realised that I too had the gift of dowsing.

On another occasion, I saw a body wrapped up in plastic. It could have been the boy the police were looking for.

Visions like this are unnerving, but I have had them all my life. It would be great to say that I carried on using spiritual knowledge, but other things intruded, and even though my life was steadier, the practice of meditation was lost in daily life.

Also, something happened to me about that time, which frightened me, and I became very sceptical about guides and channels.

I was reading for a friend when a woman's voice came through and she spoke in a foreign language. This scared me and I stopped all spiritual things immediately.

Yet even though I drifted away, spiritual insights never really left me.

∞

The following year, I moved to Melbourne to teach international students, but the job only lasted for two-and-a-half years.

Cairns drew me back, and I returned in 2011. The place had changed over the years and many shops were closed or taken over by other companies. The spiritual centre had moved from a lovely area, and I could not find it.

However, it was impossible to ignore the growing spiritual awareness within me, even though I hadn't had contact with it for a long time.

While I had been reluctant to get involved, I was drawn to a little spiritual shop in town, and I was soon meeting other spiritual people.

Another shop in one of the plazas sold alternative spiritual items, and the woman who ran it used to hold meditations every Tuesday morning.

The first time I went with a friend, but while in deep meditation I felt shivery all over, and it felt as though someone was trying to talk to me.

At first, I dismissed it, but it didn't stop, and it tried to contact me again the next time.

This time the spirit came in strong, and I saw a body drifting beneath the water with its t-shirt caught on a branch.

The spirit said this was his body, and he wanted the woman giving the meditation to know that he was dead.

When she heard what I had picked up, she was devastated, as she had passionately believed this man was alive. Two weeks later, his body was found in Lake Eacham.

I now accept that spirits of the deceased try to contact me, as I get shivery all over. This happened a few times when my ex-husband died. In the end, I had to tell him to go.

Since then, I have returned to the spiritual centre and resumed meditation. Things are happening daily, and I realise there is far more for me to learn. Where this will lead me, I do not know, but I hope it brings me closer to the source.

As I feel the energies in and around others, I am able to help. Often, this gives me an overwhelming urge to hug the person, and this seems to bring them relief.

This year, 2021 I want to start afresh. Rather than reading everyone who comes to me, I prefer to wait until I'm ready. Whether this is a reading, healing, or any other purpose.

There is beautiful spiritual energy present in each of us, and it should be used to the fullest extent possible.

Here is a wonderful story based on the true story of the Golden Buddha.

*'In 1957, an entire monastery in Thailand was being relocated by a group of monks. One day they were moving a giant clay Buddha when one of the monks noticed a large crack in the clay. ... The monk used a hammer and a chisel to chip away at the clay exterior until he revealed that the statue was in fact made of solid gold.'*[1]

Our spirits are magnificent, and when we remove the mud and cement, which surrounds us, gold appears.

We all tend to hide our true natures, especially the spiritual side of our being.

Let us wake up and free ourselves of such restrictions.

## *Spiritual Energies*

What is the spirit world? Was I transported to another world when I saw people and things from the past, and does this world exist in another dimension?

This leads to questions about other worlds. Is there just one, or do many dimensions interact with our own.

When we die, do we lose our awareness, or do we unite and return to an ocean of pure consciousness? This is an impossible question to answer.

Often, people who have had near-death experiences report having vivid memories from the

[1] *www.carolyntate.co The Golden Buddha*

afterlife, so I wonder: Is it possible we still exist in another reality?

This brings me to the question of reincarnation. I have actually experienced something like this when I was young.

## *Back in Time*

Shortly after my parents moved out of River House, they found work on a large estate in Denham, England.

The big old house was being restored, and the owner wanted help to clean and tend to the large garden. In exchange, they were given a small wage and a worker's cottage to live in.

This meant that while my mother cleaned the house, my father took care of the gardens, which needed a great deal of love and care.

When we visited for the first time, I was overwhelmed by strange feelings. It felt as though I should be on a horse instead of walking, but I had never ridden a horse in my life.

My parents lived in a cottage situated beside the stables, and as I walked in the doorway, it felt strangely familiar, as though I had spent all my life there. I even knew where the old gas lights should be and naturally looked for them.

The next day, we were given a tour of the estate by my parents. We began our tour at the stables where the horses used to be kept. Suddenly, I had a terrible vision and *saw* a young man hanging from the rafters. In horror I ran away crying and saying something like.

"It wasn't supposed to happen that way."

In my distress, I talked about losing my glove and I was looking at the ground wailing. My mother seeing the state I was in, suggested we have lunch first before we go to the big house. She took this strange behaviour of mine in her stride, but my father was baffled and a little annoyed.

The next place we visited was the main house, which was unoccupied and empty, but as I walked down the huge winding staircase, I was suddenly transported to a different time.

On the top of the stairs, there was a full-length mirror, but the reflection was not me, as my hair was black and full of ringlets, and my skin was an alabaster white.

The dress I was wearing was made of a soft, dusky pink fabric, which looked lovely.

As I looked at my reflection, sadness overwhelmed me like nothing I had experienced before, and as I didn't want to know all this, I turned away.

Walking down the stairs, I noticed paintings covering every available space possible. Some images showed men on horseback with fierce demeanours, and women who held their heads too stiff for a good pose.

One of these paintings showed a lovely female with flashing eyes. She was wearing a riding outfit and holding a crop, as though she wished to strike down the artist who was painting her picture. She looked and felt familiar, and again I rejected what I was seeing and looked away.

I heard a harpsichord playing and the chatter of female voices downstairs, and I felt I should be there with them. Then, just as I *felt* and *saw* these things, the feeling left me, and I was back in the present.

My father had just finished telling my husband about the fine paintings, which had once been on the bare walls, and the exquisite furnishings, of which he had helped to remove.

I looked around me in shock! The walls on the stairwell were bare and there was no carpet, and yet I remember both.

The sounds of music playing and women laughing had gone. Instead, there was a silence, which was unnerving. In a mad flurry of fear, I pushed past my husband and ran out of the house.

Later, when I had recovered, I told my mother about the experience, because I knew my father or husband would laugh.

Although I must admit, my husband probably would have understood if he had been on his own. Men, when they get together like to think they are beyond the supernatural or strange.

I suppose this would be put in the category of a past life experience, and this is what it felt like. As I was convinced, I had been that beautiful female with the dark ringlets and a dusky pink dress.

We found out later that a jilted lover hanged himself in the stables. I can only assume that the girl who had jilted him was the one walking down the stairs. Maybe he was a gardener's son who was not supposed to have dealings with the *gentry*.

Even my hard-headed father's attitude would have been shaken by my experience, although I am sure he would never expose his opinion of the matter.

Many people around the world believe we return to this planet to learn from our past lives.

The following chapters present some of my thoughts and ideas about the spiritual world, and since we all have different opinions, I recommend reading with an open mind.

# ***Part Two: Essays***

Before I continue, let me remind my readers. The opinions in this book are mine, and some of them may be in opposition to yours. Nevertheless, this is how I comprehend the spiritual world so please accept these differences and understand we are all different.

## *Reincarnation*

As you can see from the story *Back in Time* in part one, I have also experienced the feeling of living before. Although I'm unsure how to interpret this, it occurred.

Many cultures believe the spirit returns to earth to take on a new body, and even Christianity once held this belief.

Although this belief persisted, the powers that be suppressed them, for how could they govern the masses if people knew they would live again?

For if people had a second chance to fix the mistakes they made in this life, they would try to not make the same mistakes again.

This would mean that religious organisations and priests would not be necessary, as the fear of immediate punishment would cease to exist.

Thus, even though the subject of reincarnation was accepted in many ancient scriptures, any hint of it was carefully removed from the Bible, and in the following decades, those who believed in reincarnation were branded as evil, witches, or worse... [2]

In recent years, reincarnation has been re-investigated, and it has been proved that many children around the world remember a past life.

A respected Psychiatrist, called Ian Stevenson investigated past lives of various people around the world, see endnote... [3]

It is my belief that we return to this earth plane because we elect to do so, but if we so wish, we are free to live in any dimension or planet within this vast universe.

One purpose of our return is to correct the wrongs we did in our previous lifetime, but I am sure this is not the only reason. Our choice to return might also be related to how much we enjoyed being here. Could it be all up to us at the end, anyway?

When a person leaves this earth plane, what happens to their spirit? By accounts of near-death experiences, our energy appears to move through a

---

[2] *Reincarnation: The Missing Link in Christianity* by Elizabeth Clare Prophet. *Published August 9th, 2017, by Summit University Press (first published March 1st, 1997)*

[3] *Twenty Cases Suggestive of Reincarnation. 1966, University Press of Virginia. Ian Stevenson*

tunnel. We then meet people we have known in this lifetime, or it might be a place of respite between worlds, and what we encounter there is just an essence of their spirit.

It's possible we create this dimension by our belief system, such as some people believe Jesus will be there waiting for them and sure enough, he is. If we believe we will be met by our loved ones, I'm sure their energy will be present.

Do we create or imagine an image of what they look like here on earth and project it into that space, and since we don't want to lose all of earth's connections, this resting place may not differ from earth?

Leaving a physical form with our awareness intact we can travel to the source of energy. This source is a fabric of life itself. We call it consciousness, God, Krishna, Allah, Buddha. but it is all the same energy.

Despite this, it lacks form and can only be transformed through intent, just as we can create events by making use of our imagination.

Mentally unbalanced people may also create unformed shapes so ugly they end up living in a twilight world of nightmares.

Some of these thought-forms creep into our world and manifest unimaginable havoc, and I believe evil spirits are creations made by man from his negative energies.

This is important. Let us assume there are indeed other worlds and in those worlds are various spirits or entities. Some of these are good, while others are not so nice.

We should all remember that our light energy is our powerhouse, and it keeps each and every one of us alive.

It is my belief that a spirit should not take over an individual no matter how good it is, as it could lessen their life-force, especially if it has evil intentions.

Some spirits have much wisdom to impart, but be aware, some are not what they seem.

Whenever a person's life-force is compromised, they can suffer from a wide range of ailments and illnesses, and healing and meditation are the only means to recover.

To counteract any bad energies, visualise a powerful light flowing through and around you.

## *Butterfly Wings*

Because of strange events that have accompanied me throughout my life, I have formed a strong belief in the magical powers of the universe. I honestly believe that what one desires is not just the outcome of positive thinking.

We can achieve the impossible if we believe it can happen, and I have found that my true desires are achieved when I am not too persistent in wanting them to become reality.

Let me try to explain what I mean.

A thought is like a butterfly with iridescent wings. As it flows away from the being that gave it life, this exquisite creature pulsates with all the colours of the rainbow.

The lovely life form drifts out into the eternal energy of the universe, sometimes guided by the wishes, and hopes that accompany it.

Filled with all these thoughts and desires, it drifts on the airwaves of eternal knowledge until it lands upon the object, individual, or idea it has been directed to. Here it will live and grow and produce the wishes and desires it was intended for. These will turn into other butterflies that will flow back to the being who gave them life and rewards will flow.

As soon as the weight of hope or desire becomes too heavy, the lovely ethereal creature is dragged back into the realm of mortal existence. Once there, it drifts back to its maker and sinks into the depths of the physical realm, never to flit on wings of energy to its final paradise.

Therefore, if you have a thought, let it go. Don't hold it hostage until it dies. When your heart desires something, envision it once, then let it drift away like an iridescent butterfly. Do not continue to wish or desire or your thoughts will become negative and will never take wing to your desires.

This is the power of belief.

## *Earth Energies*

*Published in the Life magazine. September 9, 2009. by Grace Lee.*

I can remember when I was travelling with my friend; we had avoided the main tourist pathways and travelled to out of the way places where we knew others would not disturb us. Then we had pitched our tent and lived as nature intended.

This was my first encounter of living out-of-doors for any length of time and although I had undertaken such an adventure when a child, with great delight, I was dubious about this at my late age I can tell you.

Despite this, something wonderful happened to my awareness, and it was so intense that I realised how much I had left behind in my childhood.

A state of profound mindfulness came upon me, and I sensed the rain just by the look, feel, and atmosphere the trees radiated towards me.

The trees gave off an air of expectancy, which I had never noticed before. In fact, these large stately eucalypt trees reminded me of children waiting for the school bell or tea to come their way, and as the rain approached, there was a growing sense of urgency.

The birds would become more talkative and the whole place would be alive with heavenly voices as they sang their praises out to the sky.

Then just as suddenly as they had spoken there would be a palatable silence and down came the rain. It was as if they had asked the rain to come. In fact, sometimes it seemed as if this were the case, since the sky would often look clear before the storm.

Looking around me, I realised everything was alive. Plants, grass, and the very air are bursting with energy far beyond what your mind can understand.

The world has a subtle way of communicating, even if we aren't aware of it, and the bird's, insects and animals of any kind are part of this beat and are in constant unity with nature.

This energy exists within and around us, and before we can achieve enlightenment, we must re-connect with it.

Take a walk, but this time when you walk be aware of all that is around you, from a flowering tree to a bird singing. Really notice not just look, then turn away. Feel and hear these presences, smell, and taste them in your mind, and take some time to sense the living world around you. In this way, you can reconnect with nature.

## *Far Seeing and Other Things*

'{If}... the Monteganais Indians of eastern Canada wish to contact a distant relative, they go into a hut in the forest and build up the necessary psychic energy through meditation: then the relative would *hear his voice.* [4]

As children, we lived in a spatial world, where our imagination could create playmates and make imaginary worlds. We may not recollect or produce these things now, but back then they were very real. So, what happened to the reality we once knew, and what changed our childlike perceptions?

As we reach adulthood, we lose a gift, a wonderful gift, and this is to be as a little child. They were simple

---

[4] *Beyond the Occult, by Colin Wilson. Penguin books. Published: 13 January 2021*
*ISBN: 9781786783486*

days but good, because we could imagine the impossible, and magical advents were as natural as breathing.

It was quite believable to imagine getting a pushbike for Christmas and it turned up as requested. We could desire many things and they would happen to us, either in our imagined world or take on physical shape and become real.

Many primitive people from around the world have kept a childlike belief system, and it does not seem strange to *send* thoughts to a relative in another city or travel the skies with the eye of an eagle.

People used to treat shamans, witch doctors, or other gifted people as though they were magicians or gods. This still happens with psychics and healers.

Over time, the ability to connect as a spiritual being has diminished, and the mere suggestion of such abilities is often considered a form of mental illusion.

Many gifted people can see, feel, and hear what is happening to the person in front of them, so where is the proof it is a delusion?

It is pathetic to believe that just because I *know* something I am fooling myself. Especially when the *knowing* has been proved beyond doubt. I can assure you with absolute certainty that you are capable of magic.

Many gifted people use various accessories to connect with the person who has come for a reading. These can be Tarot cards, numerology, and runes, to name a few, and for a time I too used these as a way of connecting with the sitter.

If the sitter is nervous, tarot cards can help to placate them. Plus, they are a nice way to connect as they are colourful and having intuitive messages on them, which helps in the reading. I have thought of using them just for this purpose.

However, these are only a technique for connecting to the sitter's vibrational essence, for as a reader develops spiritually, they will sense, feel, and see energies and spirits swirling around the sitter.

It is well-known that there are gifted readers who have had this ability since childhood, either by the very action of being born, or by a near-death experience.

While we are not all aware of it, everyone has these gifts, and meditation can be an effective way to access them, as it allows the body and mind to rest and connects you with a higher power.

Remember, there is nothing you cannot do if you just believe. In fact, the man Jesus stated you could *move mountains if you so wished*, and he was correct.

## *Love*

Down through the mists of time gathering intensity great energies stirred, whirling, and dipping as they alighted for a while to create life.

For a while, a mere fleeting moment, great energy grew. It had no form, no limits, and no dimensions.

It is love.

Love has always existed.

Love drew breath and sighed out all creation.

Love created the universe, planets, and life itself.

Love created memory within its creations and formed all existence.

Without love, the world as we know it cannot exist. Grace Lee.

## *Thoughts*

*From spirit, through spirit, to spirit.*
*Quote by Helen Chittendon, Spiritualist*

Many strange things have happened throughout my life. From spirits, other realities, unidentified flying objects, and out-of-body experiences. Thus, I am convinced that many dimensions intermingle with ours, and in one of these dimensions a few spirits remain to watch over and interact with us. Why they remain around us, I am not sure, but they are there, and will help us if we need it.

Perhaps in some places the past and future interact, which is why I had parallel experiences. Perhaps some of these worlds are created by our imagination and dreams.

It is my belief that life continues to exist as energy no matter what happens to us. We are born with our own will and our own spiritual tasks here on this planet, and we must fulfill these tasks with the gifts we are born with. If this means we don't fulfill it this time around, we will return to this earth plane until we succeed.

The human body is a complex mechanism, which houses the bones, organs, cells, blood etc. however, life cannot exist without an invisible life-force or energy to drive it.

At this very moment, I sit on a chair, which is inert and lifeless. It does not get up and run away, for it has no spiritual essence to motivate it, and believe me I would run in the opposite direction if it did.

Within the physical form, we have vibrations that bind us together, holding the electrons and atoms of our body securely around our spiritual blueprint.

There is one theory, first suggested by Rupert Sheldrake in his book. *Morphic Resonance.* [5]

In the book, he argues that every living thing has an energy field, and this field is like a blueprint that the body copies to produce itself. This, I believe is our vibrational pattern or life-force.

If our life force is balanced, we would be perfect in every way, mentally, physically, and spiritually.

In this state, we should be able to connect with everything around us, both on the physical and spiritual level, but only a rare few have ever reached such a state of total balance.

Throughout our lives, we are constantly exposed to invisible waves of energy, known and unknown.

These waves hold a frequency that resonates within our physical bodies, and we receive information, just as an aerial receives and transmits messages to radios and TVs.

Let me explain in more detail on how I perceive this to be.

As humans, we have been led to believe that we once crawled on all fours like the animals, and over time we became erect and learned how to walk on two

[5] *Morphic Resonance: The Nature of Formative Causation. Park Street PressEdition4th Edition, Revised and Expanded Edition of A New Science of*

feet. Whether this occurred is still a matter of speculation, and even though it is taught in schools, it is still considered a theory. However, for this study, let us assume that we have always been upright beings.

Basic anatomy shows us that the spinal column connects our nerves to our lower and upper body.

Every living thing has a column of power (the spine). Meridians, as they are called in Chinese medicine, connect the spine to various parts of the body.

Meridian lines are pathways of pure energy, and these pathways connect to cores of energy spinning throughout our bodies in many areas.

These cores of energy are called chakras, and they resonate with the earth and universe.

Our chakras act as receivers, picking up the vibrations from the universe, space, and everything around us.

We are attuned to the magnetic pull of the earth by our base chakra and the pull of the planets by our crown chakra.

For example, if we sit cross-legged and erect on the ground or floor, our spine connects with the earth. By doing so, we become a human aerial that can receive messages from the earth and from space.

Thus, if our energies are balanced, it would be like being tuned into a giant aerial. In this way, we could receive information from many places, and could access knowledge from other dimensions, as well as our own. We could send thoughts and energy as well as receive them and be able to know past and future clearly.

Trees, plants, animals, humans, and everything are affected by a life energy, which vibrates through them.

If we look back at the earth from space, we can see a lovely blue haze surrounding it. This is the earth's aura. This is the earth's life energy.

We also have an aura. This can be in many colours. In fact, everything alive has this same union. Hence, the earth and the universe beyond act as a gigantic aerial, and we are the receivers.

This means that as receivers, we can also heal and be healed. What a lovely idea, and even if I am not completely correct, this is a good explanation.

## *Healing*

Healing can happen spontaneously. One woman was on her deathbed, yet she recovered. Her book is well worth reading. *Dying to be me, by Anita Moorjani* [6]

[6] *Dying to be Me. By Anita Moorjani, Wayne W. Dyer (Foreword)*

Most times, someone helps with the healing. This happened to me when I was a young woman. Around this time, I was experiencing an uncomfortable discharge. The doctor sent me to a specialist for examination and diagnosed an ulcer on my cervix. This frightened me.

My mother, a deeply religious woman was of the opinion that God could heal any disease, so she took me to a charismatic healer in Birmingham.

This man was so popular that the stadium where the event was held was full.

He talked for a while, but I don't remember what he said. Then he began healing people. He healed a man who could not walk before, and we witnessed him walk off the stage with no help.

Then he asked all the people in the audience who were sick to put their hands on, or close to, their problem. I naturally obeyed by putting my hand between my legs, and as I was embarrassed, I hid my hand under my coat.

In his prayer, he asked God to heal the sick and ailing amongst us. At that moment, a powerful energy surged through my womb, and I knew I had been

---

*Published March 1st, 2012, by Hay House (first published January 1st, 2012)*

healed. Two weeks later, the specialist told me the ulcer had gone on its own.

All healing depends on the person who has come for the treatment, as they must honestly believe they will be healed.

It is not the person who is the healer, but the universal energy flowing through them and out to the person who receives it.

Healing is not possible if there is any doubt about the healer or the recipient.

There is an intimate web of energy within and around the person, and if this energy is disrupted or broken, it will cause sickness.

Sickness can occur in the mind, emotions, or the body, and I have observed some individuals hold on to their sickness, even though they want to be healed. Why this is, I am not sure.

Our bodies possess a complex energy field, and we all have the potential to heal ourselves. There are many ways to heal ourselves and one of the most important of these is our diet. Unfortunately, many people don't bother eating healthy food and end up getting sick as a result, and we can see the effects in the growth of sicknesses such as diabetes.

Many healing remedies harmonise with our life-force, such as homoeopathic, flower essences, aromatherapy, and massage.

Every living thing is connected to a core of energy, and if we are tuned into this energy, we would be magnificent. Thus, I believe we can heal ourselves by aligning with the correct energy flow.

Meditation has many benefits in healing, as once we go to that quiet space, we can remove negative attachments easily.

This allows us to become more aware of the universal energy and gain inner peace and help us remove the blocks that prevent us from becoming a whole, healthy person.

Taking stock of your strengths allows you to rise above the negative thoughts and emotions you encounter every day.

We all have a wonderful life energy flowing through us, and as I walk with spirit and allow this energy to flow through me, I am growing and learning.

## *Light Beings*

The path to spiritual knowledge and awakening does not occur instantly, and you must be certain that you truly want to attain this state, as becoming enlightened involves tremendous responsibility.

A fully awakened being is in touch with the vibrational energy of the universe, and in this way shamans and teachers gathered knowledge and were thought of as gods.

Although we are not aware of their existence, many dimensions and worlds exist within the universe, and these can be traversed by awakened souls.

As soon as the soul awakens, everything becomes spiritually accessible to them, and when they leave this earthly plane, they will become beings of light.

The energy of a light being expands and grows to gigantic size, and the light beings we call angels have an incredible amount of energy, and this is visible to human beings as wings.

As one sets out on a spiritual journey, light beings are there to guide them. They surround us, and help us in every way, even though we may not be aware of them.

There is a source of knowledge, and as our light grows, we are connected with everything. There is a thirst for more, and the more you are given the more you are offered.

Another thing to consider is that no one person is higher than you. It may appear this way in the physical world, but on the higher spiritual plane we are all equal, and even though they have great intellect, they are no better than you.

The enlightened individual has a balanced outlook on all aspects of their life, emotional, intellectual, physical, and spiritual.

Their lives are infused with spiritual energy, which reaches out to everyone around them, and they have a greater understanding about the spiritual world.

If we connect with the light source, we too can become light beings, so stay humble and recognise this truth.

The earth plane is just one of many schools of learning. Graduates of these schools can travel dimensionally to every planet in the universe.

Where there is light, darkness cannot enter, yet sadly, dark energies inhabit dimensions close to our own. To decrease the power of dark entities, we must send spiritual light to them and ask for help from a light being.

Depression, hatred, anger, and jealousy attract dark energies into your space, and illness can follow.

The physical form cannot allow dark powers to take control, or war and strife will surely follow. Sadly, many people in high places have darkened their sphere of light and have allowed this to happen. Thus, we must let the light flow through and out to the world so we can cleanse the world of evil.

# Part Three
# Meditations

# Relaxation and Meditation

'How do I meditate?... asked of Sogyal Rinpoche's master...'
'Look, when one thought has ceased and died, before another thought has yet risen, isn't there a gap?'
'Yes,' the diplomat said. 'Prolong it, Prolong that gap. That is meditation.'
From 'The Fragrant Heavens' by Valerie Ann Worwood. [7]

In our hectic daily lives, it's difficult to relax, and meditation can be extremely beneficial for our bodies, minds, and spirits since it reduces blood pressure, boosts immunity, and enhances the physical body's ability to heal itself.

Meditation is achieving inner silence. A place where we can work on a different level to remove any blocks and problems we encounter in our daily life.

Once we see beyond the mundane, everyday physical occupations of life, we realise that we're in contact with a far greater power.

It is easy to meditate, it just takes a letting go of all the worldly thoughts.

---

[7] *'The Fragrant Heavens' by Valerie Ann Worwood. Penguin books.* Published: 31 August 2013 ISBN: 9781446464168

## *A Short Exercise in Meditation*

Find a quiet place where you will not be disturbed. Take the phone off the hook and turn off your mobile. You should stay warm if possible as the body temperature goes down when it is in this state. You can either lie down or sit. It is up to you.

Now close your eyes and try to look at your thoughts, which seem to jump around for attention like children.

Visualise or imagine a big screen like a cinema screen and as each thought comes on the screen of your mind, allow it to drift across as though it is a cloud moving across the sky.

Gradually, let the thought clouds dissolve and completely drift away. In this way, you are teaching your mind to focus on one thing at a time.

Now relax your body and feel all the tension drift away. If this is difficult at first, start at your feet and let go... relax.

Now take this sensation up the legs... and relax.

Slowly move up your body, letting each part of you... relax.

Sometimes it feels as though this will never happen and you may need to tense a muscle in a particular area and then release it. Doing this seems to unlock the muscle and allows it to relax.

Once all your muscles are released, you can float in this soft, relaxed state for as long as you like.

If you wish to bring yourself out of this state, do it gently. Do not move immediately, just lie there and allow sensations to come back to your body.

When you are ready, open your eyes and take in your surroundings.

Colours appear brighter, as if they have been washed, and your thoughts are clearer.

If you practise this small meditation each day, you will feel the stresses of life leave you. Your mind will be much clearer, and your body will feel more relaxed and fresher.

At first, it may seem impossible to achieve a peaceful state of mind, and you may feel frustrated. Remember that learning meditation takes time, but it gets better the more you practise.

When I had my spiritual experience in Darwin, I used the following meditation. In order to help me, I recorded the meditation so that I could listen to it later.

When recording the meditations, linger for a few minutes where the dots are. This will allow you to relax.

Imagination and visualisation may seem strange at first, but they are practical practices for meditation that provide a way to relax and release stress.

Visualisation is the cornerstone of all my meditations, as they are cathartic and can help you achieve inner peace.

Note: the dots represent rest periods.

## *Colour Chakra Meditation*

Find a comfortable place. You may sit or lie. If you sit, the energy will flow along your spinal column, which is conductive for a good meditation.

Close your eyes and let your body relax. Relax every part of your body, even your toes... Your feet.... your legs.... up your thighs and into your body.

Let this relaxation go through your stomach, and chest, and into your shoulders. Allow them to droop and let go of tension...

Allow the relaxation to flow down your arms and into your hands.

Let the tension go in your neck, spine, and head.

Let everything relax... take your time and allow this complete relaxation to move through your body...

Relax.... Now I want you to imagine you are in a cinema. You sit in a nice comfortable seat facing the screen. As you look at the screen, you see your thoughts jumping around like clowns. Bring in some clouds... and put every annoying thought into a cloud, and let them drift off the screen...

Stay looking at the screen and as you look you can see a lovely, pure, white light. Now imagine that the seat you are on moves and merges with the white light on the screen. You are in your film.

I want you to create your own special place; it could be on the beach or in a forest, or any place that is special to you....

Now as you sit in your special place, you are surrounded by love... feel that love surround you.... There are smells here; it could be the freshness of the plants, or the salty air of the sea. It could even be the smell of fresh bread. Just enjoy whatever you imagine in your special place....

You might hear birds singing in the sky, the sea, or the sound of trickling water... whatever sounds they are, they fill you with peace... nothing here can harm you...

You are relaxed, so just enjoy being in your special place. There are no worries, no intruding thoughts, just you... you can feel the air flowing around you and the earth or sand beneath your body... all is good there is nothing to worry you... relax for a while...

Now bring the focus back to your body and feel how relaxed it is...

I want you to picture a swirl of red energy at the base of your spine. It is a lovely letterbox red.... as it whirls around, allow this lovely red to grow until it is flooding your body... Allow it to drift through you for a while....... Imagine it flowing like water through your body...

Gradually allow the red to flow back to the base of your spine.... to cleanse and purify it imagine, you are dropping white light into it...

Now, move your attention to just below your navel. This is the sacral chakra. Imagine a pure orange light spinning around here. Send white light to purify the orange and send it out through your body.... and as before, allowing it to flow through you for a while...

Slowly bring it back to just below your navel and cleanse it once more in drops of white light....

The next chakra dwells in your mid-section and is called the solar plexus chakra. It is a wonderful gold. Purify it with pure white light and allow this lovely golden colour to flood your body for a while... Let it engulf you and flow through you... Slowly allow it to flow back to your solar plexus, and to make sure it is pure, send drops of white light to it...

You reach the heart, this chakra is green, a wonderful magical green, send drops of white inside and allow the magical green to fill your body... this is love, and it floods through you and out to all.... feel this connection of love with everyone...

This is a powerful chakra as it connects with every living thing on the planet. If there is no love, there would be no life... take time to absorb this light........ then gradually bring the lovely green back to your heart...

The light in your throat is blue, a lovely sky blue called the throat chakra. It is the colour of healing and the seat of truth. Cleanse the blue with drops of lovely white light and then let it flow through and around you for a while....... feel it penetrate every part of you and heal any hurts within... finally bring it back to your throat.

The third eye chakra sits between your eyebrows at the centre of your head. It is indigo. Here is the place where you make your decisions and also the place of intuition and a link with spirit.

Cleanse it by sending white light through it... then send this wonderful colour out through your body....

Allow this energy to flow.... to allow your connections to open and connect with your intuition... take time....

Now bring this light back to your third eye and allow it to swirl with indigo energy...

The pure white light of the crown chakra whirls at the top of your head. This is a connection with all there is... this energy keeps you connected with the universal energy. It is a pure... Allow it to flow down your spine and fill your being... visualise it flowing up and down your spine.... cleansing and connecting you with spirit... Stay with this white light for a while....

Finally, bring the crown chakra back to your crown and relax... you are clear...

It is time to come home... Slowly leave your special place and return to the cinema... take time.... come back and gradually feel your body once more.... then open your eyes.

Thank you.

## *A Crystal Meditation*

Find a quiet place where there are no distractions. If you can, sit with your spine erect so you are aligned with the earth and sky**...**

If you find it hard to do this, find a place to lie down. It must be peaceful, with no disturbances.

Relax your body... find any tense spots and tighten them, then let relax... breathe a few deep breaths... then just be... Now it is time to go to the crystal pyramid.

In front of you is a lovely rainforest... There are many beautiful vines on the trees. There is a path which leads upwards follow this...

The right side of the path has a bubbling creek ... and water flowing over rocks that are covered in moss....

As you walk along the path, you realise there are many waterfalls cascading down the creek. Look around you... one vine covered tree is covered in lovely red flowers and produces a sense of peace within you....

As you continue your walk, you notice the ground is covered with orange flowers, which look something like pansies... they are everywhere...

You see another a vine covered tree that has flowers, which look like yellow trumpets... and amid all this colourful splendour is the vivid green of the forest... take some rest to contemplate this wonderful rainforest...

The smell of the rainforest is sweet and alive... and birds call out to you... and as you walk up the path, you see a Kingfisher sitting on a branch... Its feathers are as blue as the sky...

As you look up, you can see a lovely Violet purple haze... and as you near, you realise this light is coming from the very top of the mountain... within its glow is a crystal pyramid that reflect the light in a prism of colour...

Walk toward the crystal pyramid...

The crystal pyramid has a doorway on one side of it... enter this place now...

Within the pyramid is a raised seat... to reach it you have to climb three steps... it's a swivel seat and it can move in any direction.

When you reach the seat, sit down... shining down from the top of the pyramid is a beam of pure white light and it shines down upon you...

As you look, you realise that in each corner of the pyramid are tall beings... each being represents the four elements: earth, fire, air, and water...

Turn the chair to the elemental being on your left... this is earth... this entity works on the physical and earthly part of your being... he can help you with all the mortal elements within your life... He is energy... ask him if he has any physical advice to impart to you.... wait... you may hear his words in your mind... or you may receive a vision... sometimes gifts are given from these beings... wait... whatever you receive is right for you...

Now turn to the being on your right this is fire... fire is heat... He is a guardian of your sensual energy, and he gives you strength... he lights your physical self... he is a flame which burns within us... this being can help you control anger or sensual issues that may bother you.... wait.... you may receive some advice...

Swivel your seat around and face your left corner... this being is composed of air... she is there to guide you on your spiritual journey... she is an element you cannot see, yet you know she exists, just as the spiritual essence which is within you... ask for any help you need in your spiritual life... she may give you a gift or words of wisdom... wait... and receive...

On your right is water.... she is the emotional aspect within your being... let her love flow through you like water... if you have any emotional issues let her solve them and pour water over them...

Finally, thank these elemental beings and let the light from above flow through you and cleanse you... wait... remember, you are a being of light... keep the light within and around you as you descend from your seat...

It is now time to leave the lovely crystal pyramid....

When you are outside, you see the violet light has formed a path down the mountain... walk this path home...

Remember, you are safe and protected... when you are ready... come back to the physical world open your eyes and stretch.

## *Grace Lee*

Grace Lee has been interested in writing and other forms of art since she was a child. However, her writing did not take off until she began her memoir in her early sixties, which gave her a continued interest in the art of storytelling.

Grace has written several short stories, which were published in various magazines.

A prize was awarded for her bush poem *Possum's Lament,* which was published in the Cairns Tropical Writer's, Category Five.

She is a mother of five children, several grandchildren, and many great-grandchildren, and reckons there is much in her life still to do.

Grace has also written works of non-fiction and several children's books. These can be found on kindle and google books.

*An Open Door*

*An Open Door*

L - #0195 - 081221 - C0 - 229/152/7 - PB - DID3222340